Made in United States
Orlando, FL
01 June 2024

47429741R00055